Copyright © 2019 by Kristen Halverson

All rights reserved.

No part of this book may be reproduced in any form or by any electronic or mechanical means including information storage and retrieval systems, without permission in writing from the author. The only exception is by a reviewer, who may quote short excerpts in a review.

This book is a work of fiction. Names, characters, places, and incidents either are products of the author's imagination or are used fictitiously. Any resemblance to actual persons, living or dead, events, or locales is entirely coincidental.

Cover Art and Interior Illustrations by Mariana Garcia Piza

Book Layout by Indie Publishing Group

Hardcover: ISBN-9781087801797

Library of Congress Control Number: 2019914647

14104 225th Street

Elkader, Iowa 52043

First Printing: December 2019

Printed in the United States of America

For Ruby and Rum Tum

For all the cello musicians around the world

Once upon a time there was a musical cat named Ruby, who loved the cello.

Every night, she listened to her favorite cello music, and read books about famous composers.

Ruby had grown up playing the piano but longed to learn how to play a string instrument.

After school, Ruby listened to the Meow Music Group. They played all types of music, and were famous around town because of their fun winter concert. It always made everyone smile. As she watched them perform, Ruby dreamed of learning how to play the cello. Her goal was to become part of the Meow Music Group one day.

Her best friend was a cat named Moon Tune. He played in a jazz band. Moon Tune toured the world playing the bass. He had grown up playing the cello, and always encouraged Ruby to follow her dreams of learning how to play the cello.

Moon Tune meowed, "You need to talk with Cat's Music Land. They are an awesome music store. They have some amazing cellos and music teachers. I can help you learn the cello too!" Ruby said, "Great, I will start looking in the morning."

The next day arrived, and Ruby began her journey to Cat's Music Land by walking through Cat City Park. As she passed by the Cat City Pool, she noticed an old cello.

There was a sign that read," Free for any cool cat!" As Ruby crept up to the cello, she noticed that there were several holes in it.

She dashed home to tell Moon Tune about her cool cat treasure. Ruby shouted, "Moon Tune, I found a cello!" Moon Tune said, "I knew you would find one at Cat's Music Land."

Ruby said, "No, I found the cello in Cat City Park. It is not in the best shape!" Moon Tune said, "What do you mean?" Ruby replied, "It needs to be repaired!"

Moon Tune told Ruby not to waste her time with a broken cello, and that she needed to visit Cat's Music Land.

Ruby went to bed dreaming about the broken cello as she had her heart set on fixing it. The next morning, she looked through the phone book to find a store that could repair the cello. Ruby meowed, "Ah, here is place called, Cello Repair Land! This is just what I need!"

As Ruby made her way to Cello Repair Land, the sky became very dark. Suddenly, she saw a huge lightning strike in the sky as she reached the cello. Ruby crawled inside the gigantic holes of the cello until the storm passed.

She found a small yellow piece of paper where she was laying. Ruby picked up the note with her tiny paws. It read, "For Ruby, remember to always follow your heart." Ruby thought to herself that the cello must have belonged to another cat named Ruby.

It looked as though, it was going to start raining again, so Ruby snapped some photos of the cello to show Moon Tune and Cello Repair Land. When Ruby returned home, Moon Tune was waiting for her. He said, "Did you find out how much it will be to repair the cello?" Ruby said, 'No, I got caught in a bad thunderstorm! Also, I found a note inside the cello that had my name on it."

Moon Tune replied, "Let me see that note!" Ruby said, "It could have belonged to another cat named Ruby." Moon Tune replied, "This makes me curious! Now, I want to see this old cello. We should go look at it together, and then we will visit Cello Repair Land."

The next day, they ventured to the park to look at the cello. Once again, the sky got dark as they crossed the street near Cat City Park. Ruby cried, "Oh no, it looks like another thunderstorm!" Moon Tune said," We are going to get soaked!" Ruby replied, "We can hide in the cello! It kept me warm during the last storm!"

As Ruby and Moon Tune hid inside the cello, they watched the rain drops fall around them. Moon Tune said, "This was a great idea! I never imagined I would be hiding in a cello! This is really fun!" Ruby meowed, "I told you that this cello was special."

When the storm passed, Moon Tune took a closer look at the broken cello. He told Ruby that it needed to be thrown away. He meowed, "Ruby, there is no way that anyone could ever fix this cello! It can never be played again! Don't even waste your time with Cello Repair Land. You must find a new cello!"

Ruby took one final look at the cello. She whispered, "Goodbye, special cello. Thank you for keeping us safe during the bad storm. I hope another cat gives you a chance to play again."

Moon Tune saw some friends of his in the park, so he walked quickly to catch up with them. Ruby soon heard a loud cello sound. She quickly looked back to see where the music was coming from in the park. Her eyes caught the broken cello, and it had been magically been repaired.

Ruby saw glowing musical notes dancing all around her in the wind too. She meowed, "Moon Tune, slow down! Do you hear the amazing cello music?" Moon Tune replied, "Ruby, you must be dreaming again. I told you to forget about that old cello!" Ruby meowed,"I know but something awesome has happened to the cello!"

Moon Tune turned around, and ran back to Ruby. He said, "Ruby, what is this? Did you have a cello delivered to the park?" Ruby said, "No, Moon Tune! This is the broken cello. Look, read this note!"

Moon Tune meowed, "Ruby, this cello was magically restored because the Legend of Meow Cello! I heard about it from the Meow Music Group."

Ruby replied, "What legend?" Moon Tune said, "The Legend of Meow Cello says that when a cat shows kindness to an old cello, it will play music for them again." Ruby shouted, "This is a miracle! It is the prettiest cello that I have ever seen!"

Moon Tune called out to some of his Cat City Park friends to carry the magical cello home with them. When they returned, Moon Tune gave Ruby her first cello lesson. As she practiced every day, Ruby purred into the cello.

Ruby meowed, "I love playing this cello. It sounds like cat heaven to me! It is so beautiful! Moon Tune, do you think I could be ready for the Meow Music Concert?" Moon Tune said, "Yes, you will be outstanding! They love having new members to the group. I will introduce you to them tomorrow."

The Meow Music Group loved meeting Ruby. They invited her to start rehearsing with them the next day for their winter concert. She practiced morning, noon and night to prepare for the event. The special day soon arrived, and all the cool cats from their town came to see them. Ruby opened the concert with a special Bach tune.

After they finished their last song, Ruby said, "Moon Tune, thank you for helping me learn this incredible cello. My dreams have come true!" Moon Tune meowed," Ruby, the Legend of Meow Cello came true because of your kind heart, and your hope to make this cello play music again!"

www.ingramcontent.com/pod-product-compliance
Lightning Source LLC
Chambersburg PA
CBHW042019090426

42811CB00015B/1688